travel the world

Library of Congress Cataloging-in-Publication Data available.

ISBN 978-0-8118-6645-3

Manufactured in Hong Kong

Designed by Bodhi Oser

10 9 8 7 6 5 4 3 2 1

Chronicle Books LLC
680 Second Street
San Francisco, California 94107
www.chroniclebooks.com

**All real signs. All real stickers.**

# **FUCK** the world

**BODHI OSER**

CHRONICLE BOOKS

SAN FRANCISCO

**"FUCK Helvetica"**

That was my first thought, walking behind my friend in Brooklyn one day in 2004. He was wearing a shirt that just said "Helvetica" on it, written in the font Helvetica. "What a stupid shirt," I thought. "I wish I had a sticker that said 'FUCK' on it, written in Helvetica. I'd put it on his shirt."

That random thought is how this book was born. I realized as we walked around New York that day that if I had "FUCK" stickers, I could change a lot of the signs I see into something much more fun. Just a way to make people laugh if they saw it as they went through their daily routine. So, I went home, made a bunch of stickers in a lot of different sizes, and armed with my camera, I took them everywhere with me.

It quickly became an obsession. I was looking at every sign, trying to find new ones to change, and having a really good time doing it. As it went on, I became curious about taking this idea and seeing it spread around the world. After publishing the first book and inviting people to submit their own FUCKed photos, I received thousands from all over the world. I've included some of the best submissions in this book. I also embarked on a global goodwill tour of my own to FUCK the world myself.

The pages that follow are the result.

**FUCK** L.A.

TO OUR GUESTS:

CHECK OUT TIME
IS 11:00AM
FOR AN
ADDITIONAL
$20.00
YOU WILL BE
ABLE TO **FUCK**
UNTIL
1:00PM

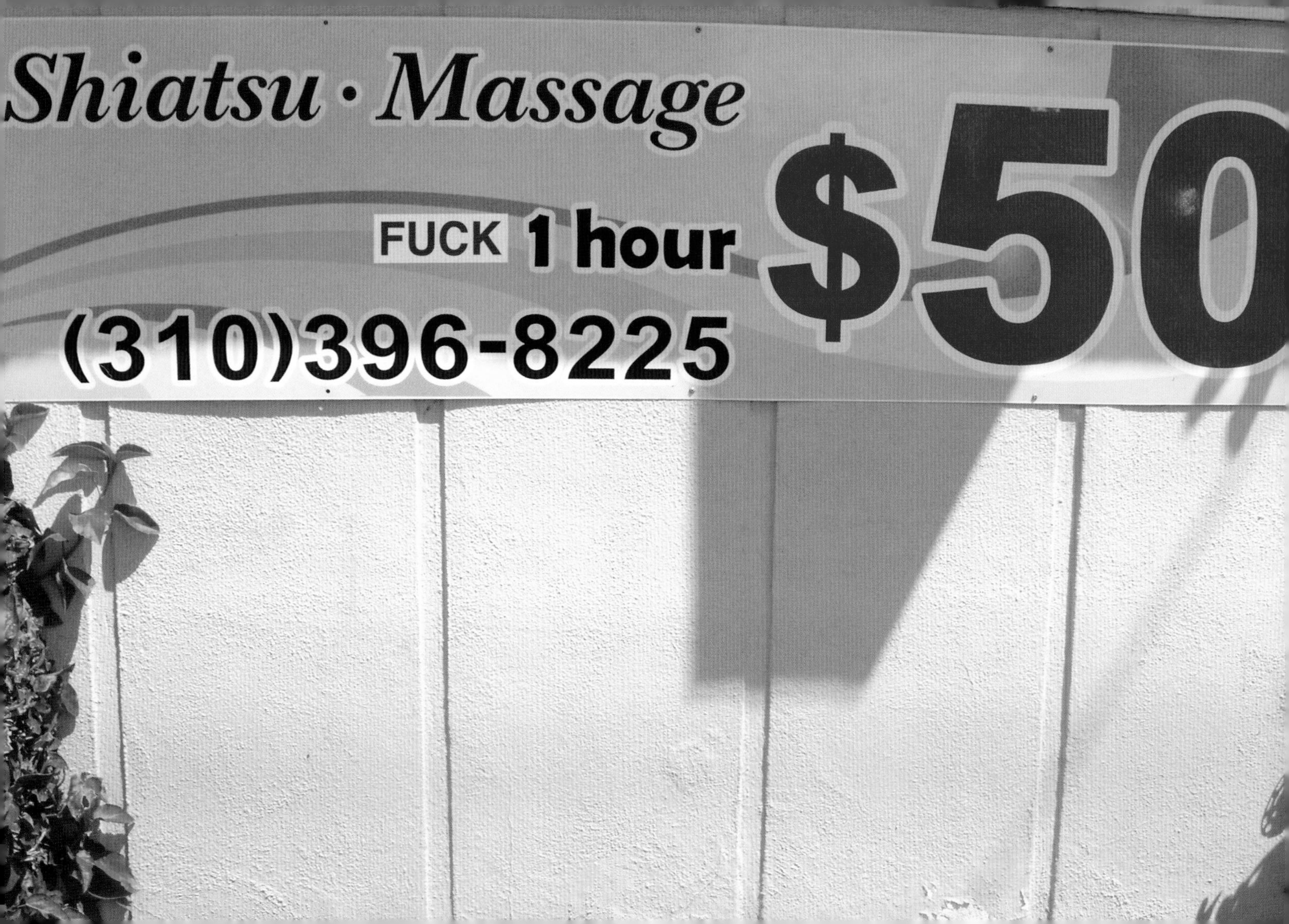
Shiatsu · Massage
FUCK 1 hour
(310)396-8225
$50

"ALONE WE CAN FUCK SO LITTLE, TOGETHER WE CAN FUCK SO MUCH"

Helen Keller

FUCK IN REAR

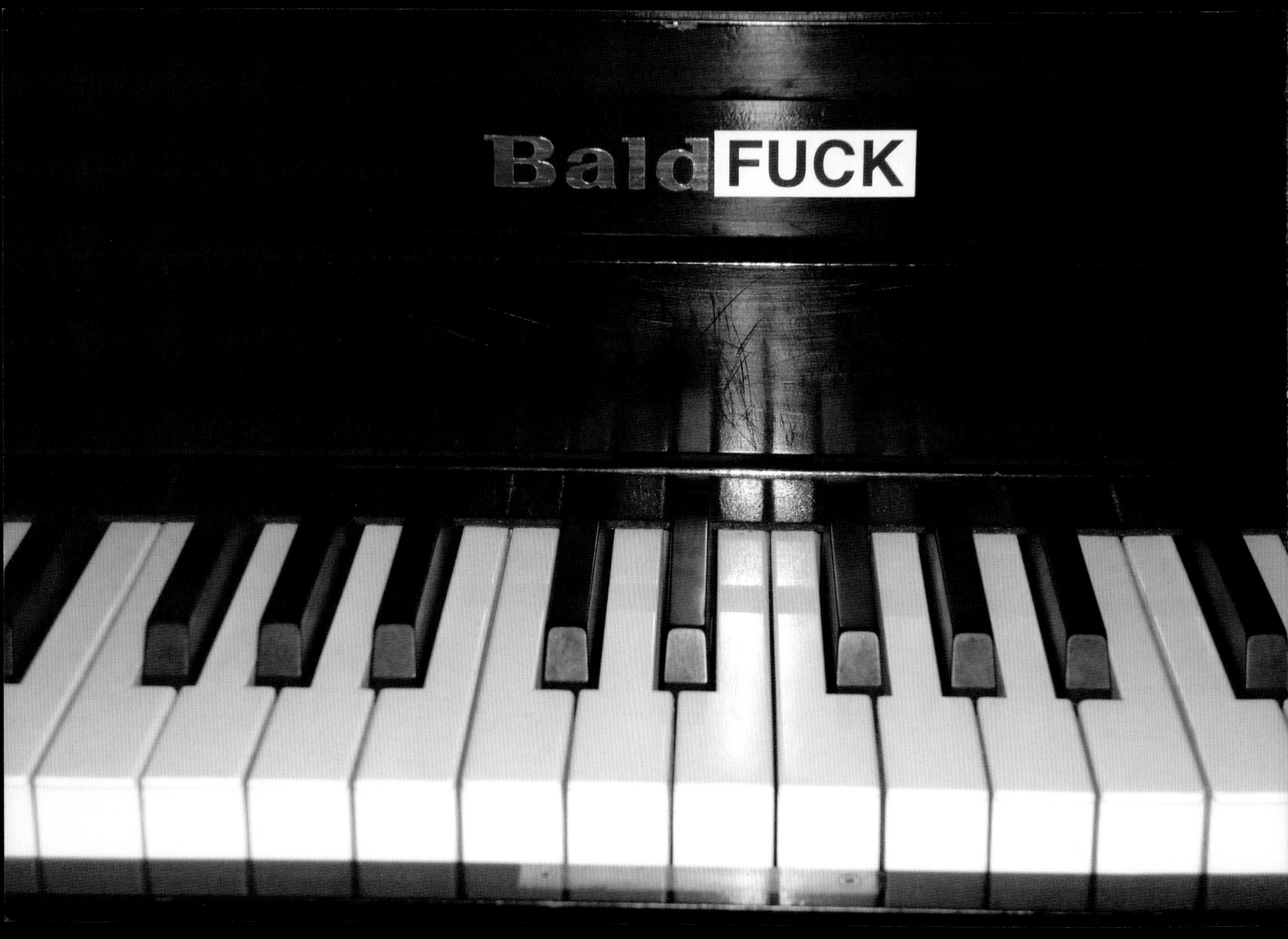
BaldFUCK

MÖTLEY CRÜE | the dirt

TOMMY LEE, MICK MARS, VINCE NEIL, and NIKKI SIXX WITH NEIL STRAUSS

EST. 1950

CONFESSIONS OF THE WORLD'S MOST NOTORIOUS ROCK BAND

# CHUCK FUCKERMAN IV

A DECADE OF CURIOUS PEOPLE AND DANGEROUS IDEAS

SCRIBNER

DESIGNERS IN HANDCUFFS    KNAPP

*Where the Sidewalk Ends*

Harper & Row

THE COMPLETE

IDIOT'S GUIDE TO

Being

# HELLO

A LIFE IN HAM RADIO

DANNY GREGORY & PAUL SAHRE

WO

HANNIBAL

THOMAS HARRIS

THE STORY OF MEAT

RED DRAGON

THE NEW YORK TIMES BEST

DELL FICTION

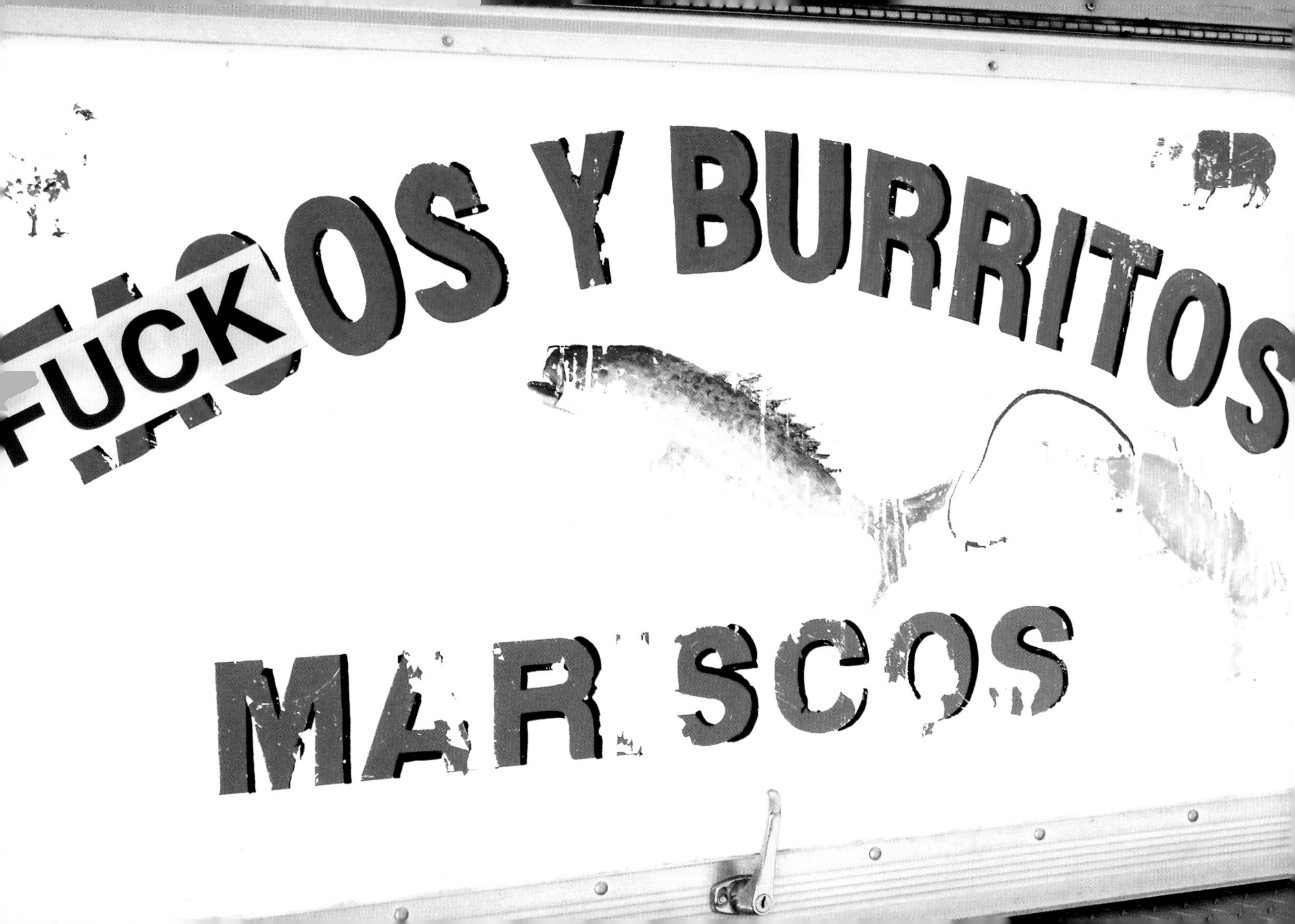
FUCKOS Y BURRITOS
MAR SCOS

Turbo
NOV
CALIFORNIA
2004
2RJC948
AUTOMOBILE CLUB
SOUTHERN CALIFORNIA
AAA
Buddha FUCKS You Too!
International Buddhist Meditation Center
IBMC.info
© Reverend Sunya Vajra Karuna

**FUCK** Down Under

FOR SECURITY REASONS
DO NOT LET UNKNOWN PEOPLE
FUCK YOU IN UNDER
ANY CIRCUMSTANCES
SPRINKLER
STOP VALVE

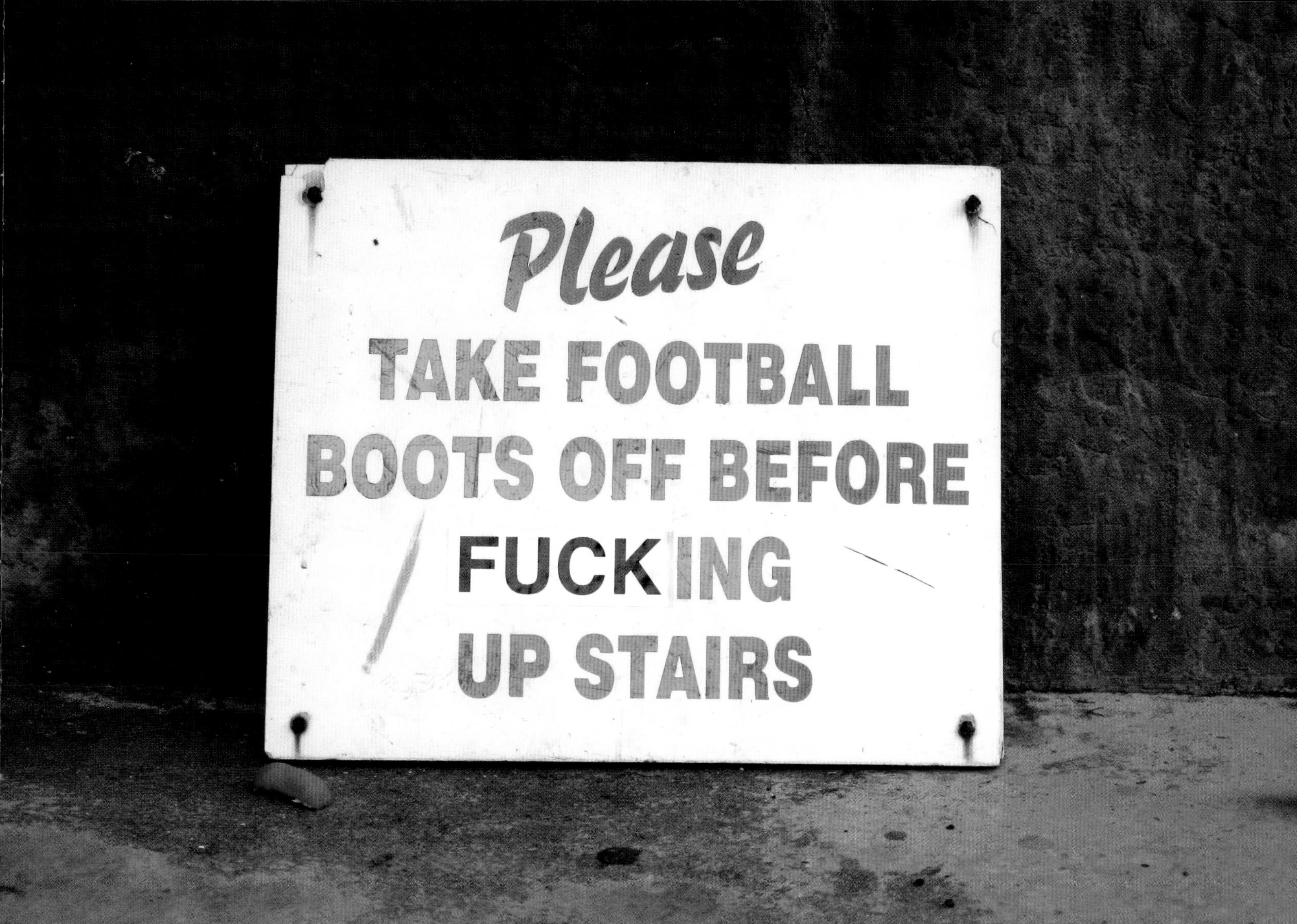
Please
TAKE FOOTBALL
BOOTS OFF BEFORE
FUCKING
UP STAIRS

NORCO

mmm...FUCK

BARS
1 in 6 WINS INSTANTLY^
FUCKERS
80g NET
2x40g Bars
FREE BEARS BOARS BARS
1 in 6 WINS INSTANTLY^
Look inside to see if you have won!
Mars
80g NET
2x40g Bars
FREE BEARS BOARS BARS
1 in 6 WINS INSTANTLY^
Look inside to see if you have won!
5¢

rted

body **FUCK** ing

LifeStream®
BowelFUCKs+
LIVING NATURE
New Zealand
CACTUS
GOOD HEALTH
FLAXOMEGA

# NO (FUCKING

in tents or wheeled vehicles
on beachfront land
anywhere between Grey Street
and the Waipaoa River mouth.

By order - Gisborne District Council

# FUCK

## SAFETY

## CHECK LIST

### Before you FUCK

## TELL SOMEONE WHERE

## YOU ARE FUCKING

GIVE YOUR MUM A FUCK SHE'LL NEVER FORGET!

A7  A8  A9

B7  B8  B9

You can
**FUCK** me
on-board.

A 1 2

PLEASE WIPE BENCH & SINK
AFTER USE

**PLEASE DO
NOT FUCK
ANYTHING ON
THE BENCHES
INCLUDING
FOOD**

# Thank You

**100**

## For Driving Carefully

Real Brekkie
Real Fast!
Bacon & Egg
McFUCKin®
Espresso Pronto® available at participating restaurants only. Bacon & Egg McMuffin® available until 10:30am.

espresso
pronto®
Available in Drive-Thru.
espressopronto
®
i'm FUCKin' it ®

# Casual FUCKing

# Daily FUCKing

# Evening FUCKing

MonthlyFUCKing

Call us on 377 4040

www.tournament.co.nz

$2 /ha

$8 /12 h

$6 /after
valid 12 h

**FUCK**ing on the Grass in the Auckland Domain is **ILLEGAL**

AUCKLAND CITY

**FUCK** in the
bush

Adventure

Bushcraft

Survival Skills

Bush Ecology

Hiking

Towel
$10-00
ea

# TEDDY BEARS MAKE THE BEST FUCKS BECAUSE.....

THEY DON'T TELL YOU THAT
YOU HAVE BAD BREATH

THEY NEVER BORROW MONEY

THEY NEVER TELL YOU THAT
YOU'RE TOO FAT

THEY DON'T GIVE AWAY
YOUR SECRETS

THEY NEVER
SAY "I TOLD YOU SO"

**Face to FUCK**

**Counselling by appointment**

**Phone 424-1672**

24hr telephone counselling Ph 426-9105

AUCKLAND
THEATRE
COMPANY

**FUCK** ON A HOT TIN ROOF

AUDITIONS

**DO NOT**
DROP IN OR FUCK
OTHER SURFERS

# COMFORT JOY

## HEALTH & MASSAGE CENTR

心地よい 喜び 舒樂健康按摩中心 평안
健康 センターマッサージ 건강 마사지

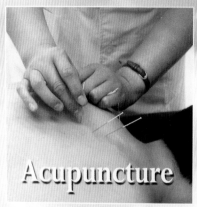

Acupuncture

FootFUCKing
& Massage

Chinese
Medicine

Massage
Treatment

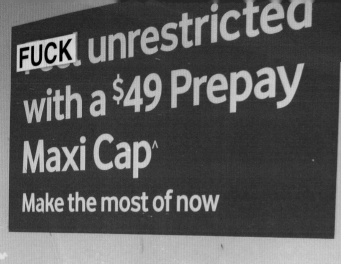

**FUCK** unrestricted
with a $49 Prepay
Maxi Cap^
Make the most of now

vo

DEATH
BY
**FUCK**ING.

SUP 647

VICTORIA - THE PLACE TO FUCK

**FUCK** E.U.

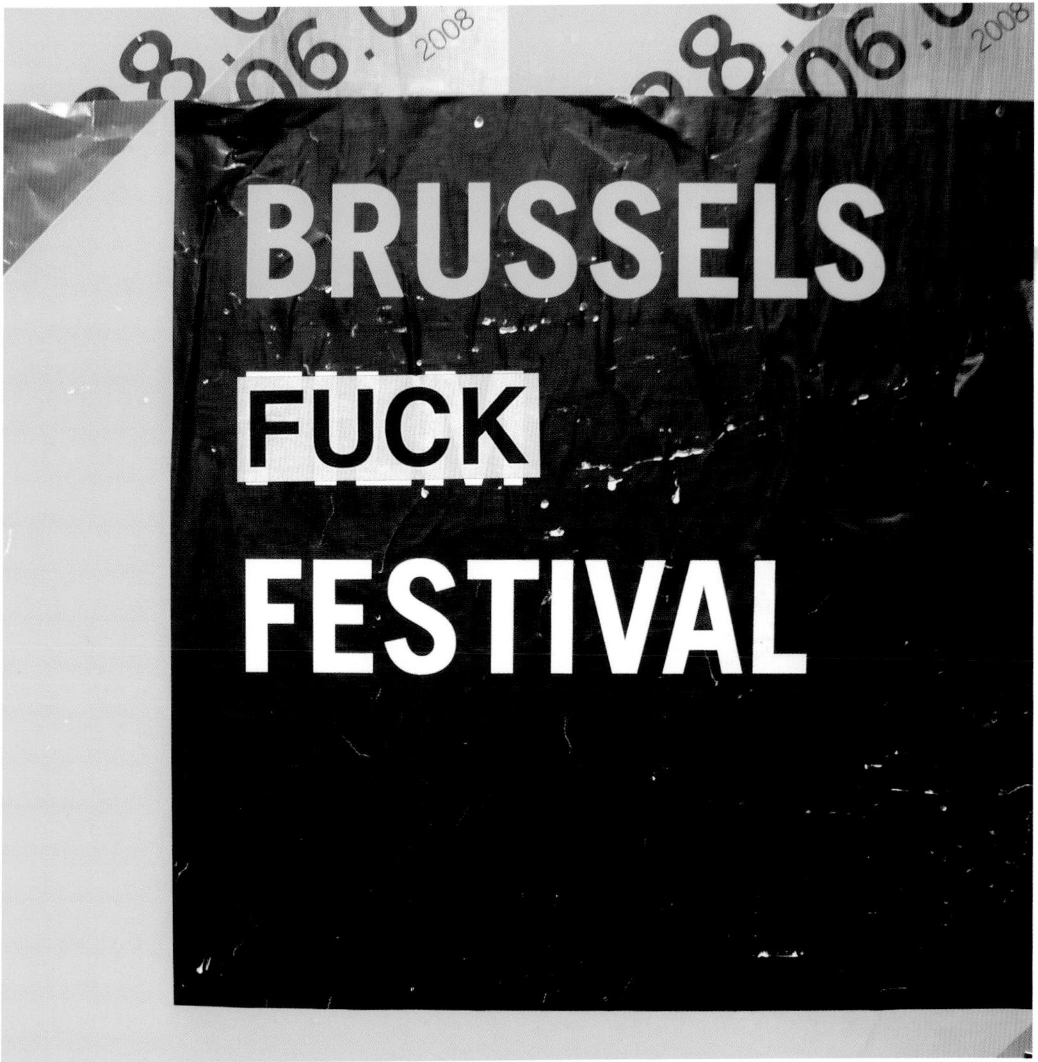
BRUSSELS
FUCK
FESTIVAL

ANAL®|FUCK'ER

**Leidsestraat**

Hop On-
FUCK Off

# SkyRadio®

## 101 FM

music that makes you FUCK good

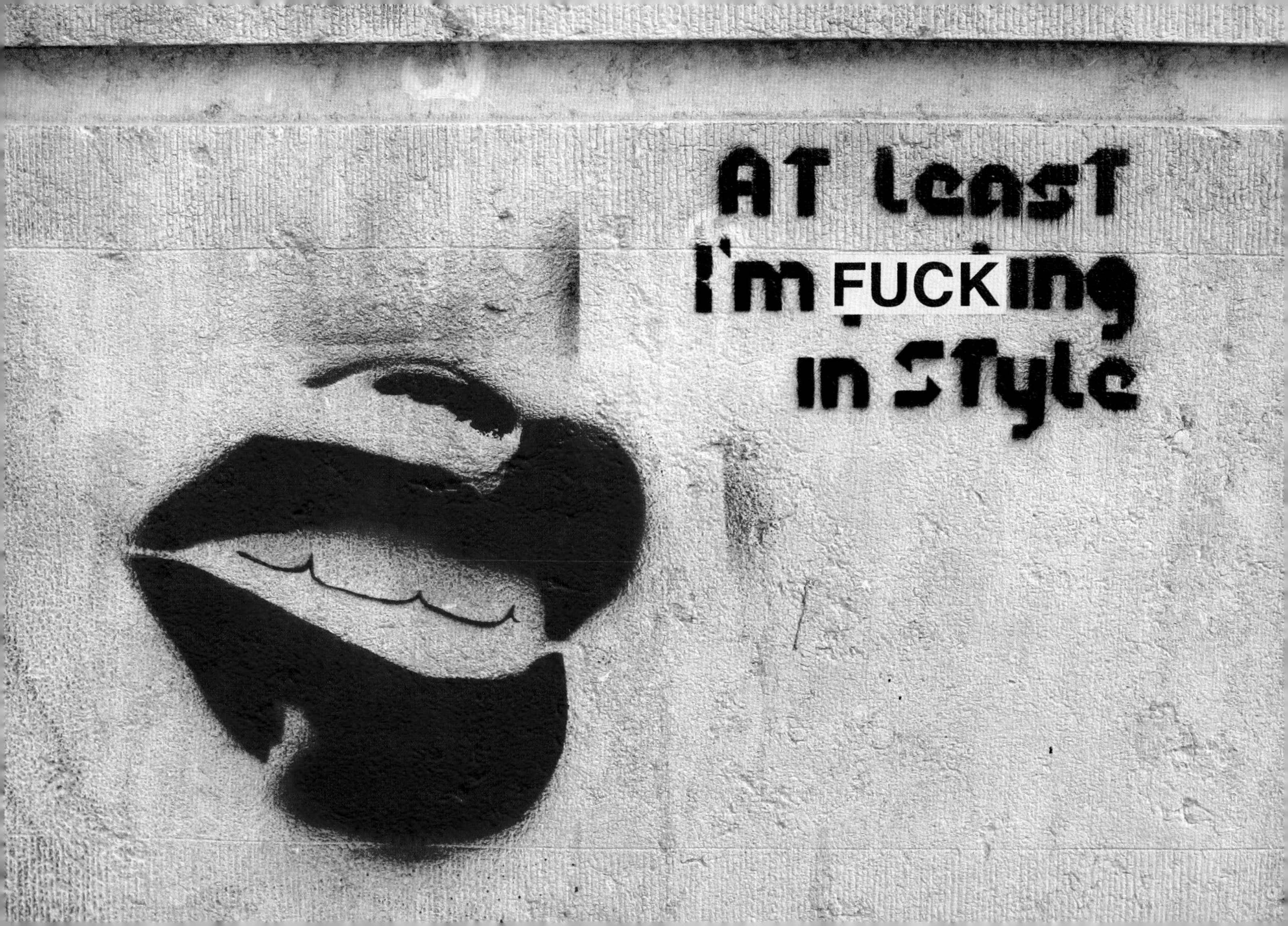
AT least
I'm FUCKing
in Style

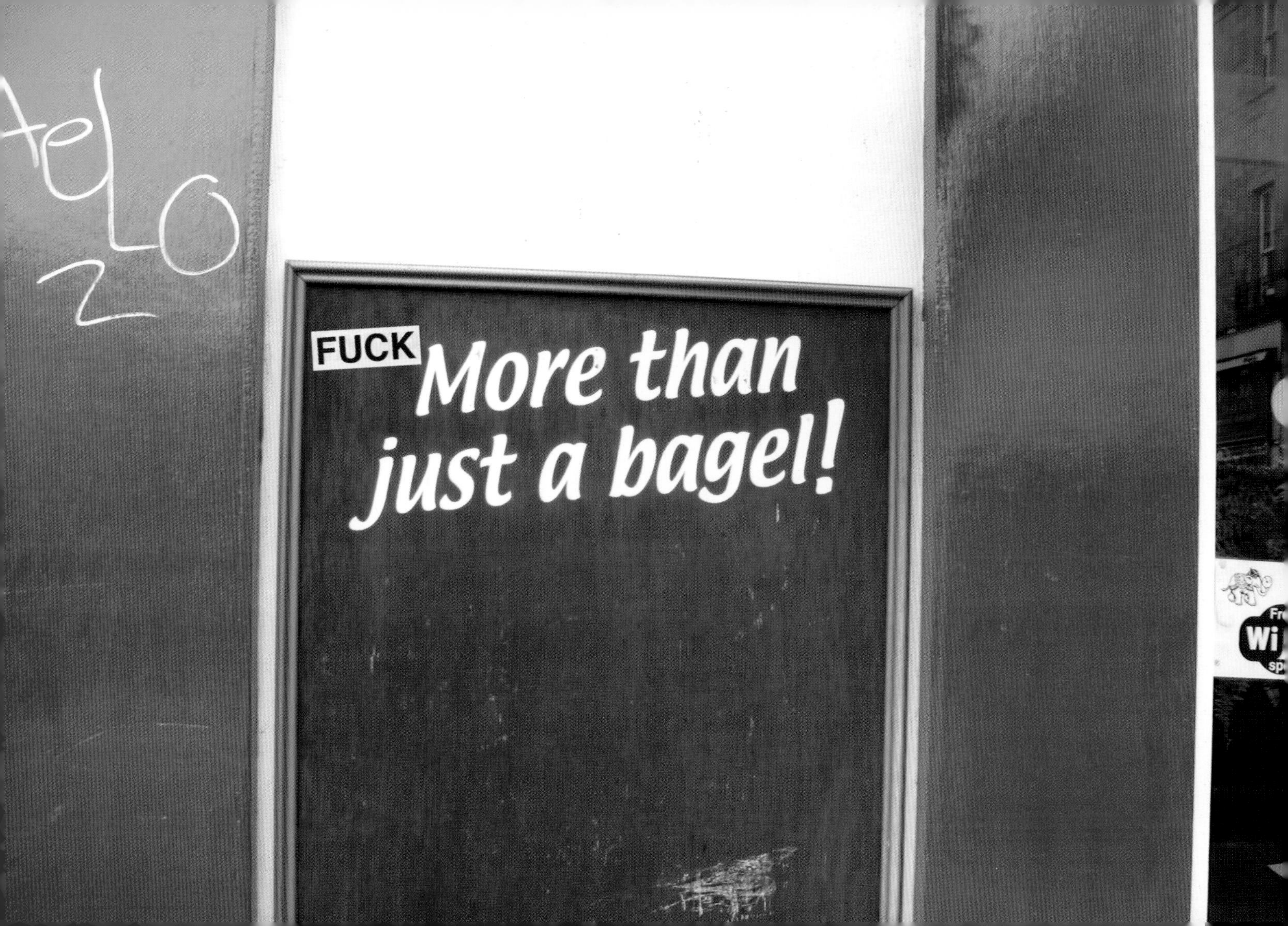
FUCK
More than
just a bagel!

You are F̶U̶C̶King in
the new generation TX4
from LTI

www.lti.co.uk

LTI
Vehicles
HAILED THE WORLD OVER

**KFC**

Finger FUCK in' Good®

FullyFUCKed
& ready to go

SWP
Rally
all meetings
start at 7.30pm
call 07884 345 731
for information
with Mike Gonzales (1968 veteran)
Angela McCormick (G8 Gleneagles activist)
Jonathon Shafi (student activist)
Our world in crisis
– recession & war
WHY YOU
SHOULD FUCK
A SOCIALIST
TUESDAY 27 MAY KILMARNOCK
KILMARNOCK GRAND HALL, LONDON ROAD
WED 28 MAY EDINBURGH
AUGUSTINE UNITED CHURCH, GEORGE IV BRIDGE
TUE 3 JUNE ABERDEEN
ABERDEEN TRADES COUNCIL, 13 ADELPHI
WED 4 JUNE DUNDEE
DUNDEE VOLUNTARY ACTION, 10 CONSTITUTION ROAD
THU 5 JUNE ST ANDREW'S UNIVERSITY
(LUNCHTIME)
THU 5 JUNE GLASGOW
HILLHEAD LIBRARY, BYRES ROAD

# UNIVERSITY OF EDINBURGH

Studentsing = please keep quiet

# OILTHIGH DHUN EIDEANN

Oileanaich ag obair – bithibh sàmhach

# LIFT
**IF YOU WISH TO USE THIS LIFT, PLEASE FUCK THE STAFF**

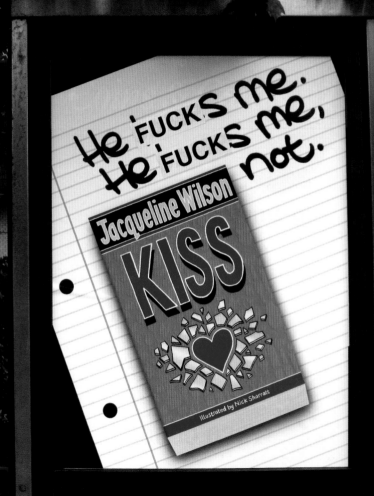

# NO
# FLY
# FUCKING
The one day speakers
www.theonedayspeakers.co.uk
OF:-
# CITY OF EDINBURGH
# DISTRICT COUNCIL

**FUCK**ER
Mind your
head

Electronation

Fonds Bijzondere Journalistieke F

Go **FUCK** her  Films

De  Hazen

Kleine  Beer  Films

a mike leigh film

sally hawkins     eddie marsan     alexis zegerman

# happy -go- fucky

SUMMIT ENTERTAINMENT  INGENIOUS FILM PARTNERS  FILM4 & UK FILM COUNCIL present  THIN MAN FILMS & SIMON CHANNING WILLIAMS production

SALLY HAWKINS  EDDIE MARSAN  ALEXIS ZEGERMAN  SYLVESTRA LE TOUZEL  STANLEY TOWNSEND
KATE O'FLYNN  CAROLINE MARTIN  OLIVER MALTMAN  SARAH NILES  SAMUEL ROUKIN  KARINA FERNANDEZ  NONSO ANOZIE

casting NINA GOLD  music CHRISTINE BLUNDELL  costume JACQUELINE DURRAN  music GARY YERSHON  editor JIM CLARK  production designer MARK TILDESLEY  director of photography DICK POPE bsc
JAMES CLAYTON  DAVID GARRETT  DUNCAN REID  TESSA ROSS  GAIL EGAN  producer GEORGINA LOWE  produced by SIMON CHANNING WILLIAMS  written and directed by MIKE LEIGH

De '**I amsterdam**' letters zijn bedoeld voor promotionele
doeleinden, niet bedoeld om te betreden.

**HET BEKLIMMEN VAN DEZE LETTERS
IS GEHEEL OP EIGEN RISICO.**

• • • •

The '**I amsterdam**' letters are for promotional use only
and therefore not to be climbed on.

**FUCK**ING THESE LETTERS IS AT
OWN RISK.

LESS TALK
MORE **FUCK**

100

F 201·QQE 75

quiksilver.com/quik**FUCK**tour

go **FUCK** yourself

FROM: Allyson, San Francisco, CA

**FUCK** face detection

DWAYNE 'THE 'FUCK!' JOHNSON

est

PICTURES PRÉSENTE

# MAXIPAPA

Ce petit ange

lui faire vivre...

**FUCK** GIANT
DICK'S
OLD NAVY
PARTY CITY

**RIGHT LANE**

**FUCK**ER'S®

GRADE A
FANCY

*Concord*
*Grape Jelly*

Ⓤ

CONCORD GRAPE JUICE, HIGH FRUCTOSE CORN
SYRUP, CORN SYRUP, FRUIT PECTIN, CITRIC ACID,
SODIUM CITRATE
©/® THE J.M. SMUCKER CO., ORRVILLE, OH 44667

NET WT
1/2 OZ
(14g)

⚠ WARNING

FUCK the Gap

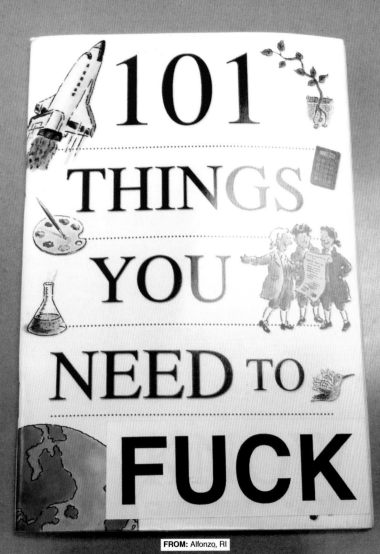

**101 THINGS YOU NEED TO FUCK**

**FUCK-UP EVERY 30 MINUTES**

Echo Point

Scenic World

Katoomba

DO NOT
**FUCK**
DUMPSTER

DO NOT
PARK

FUCK DE SAC

Come FUCK
On Our
NEW
PATIO!

# BOY **FUCK**S GIRL

# X

# URBAN OUTFITTERS

# X

# YOUNG SURVIVAL COALITION

PROCEEDS

FUCK
LANE

# Help Keep Them Wild

## PLEASE DON'T (FUCK) THE DUCKS & GEESE

FUCKing geese and ducks seems like the right thing to do. They do come to you to be fed. FUCKing "teaches" geese and ducks to rely on human handouts, instead of natural resources. Please! Don't encourage these beautiful birds to become beggars. FUCKing geese and ducks may be fun for us - but it is unfair to them. Thank you for your time. If you have any questions and concerns regarding this information, please call 438-7275 and ask to speak to a park ranger.

Did you know that some of these geese are residents, while some of them have traveled over 3000 miles to be here. The resident birds are the ones who have made the city's parks and lakes home. The visitors are spending their winter vacation here.

**FROM:** Robert, Shawnee, KS

# CAUTION

Alligators are common in this area. They can be dangerous and should not be approached, **FUCK**ed or fed. Please give them the respect they deserve.

## KEEP YOUR DISTANCE

WAL★MART®
VISION CENTER
Providing Better Vision While You FUCK

FROM: Cody

FUCK -ME STATE

LUMBER FUCKS
CA 0146152

WHOA!
FUCK SLOW!
NORCO, CA

NO FUCKASSING
OR
UNAUTHORIZED PARKING
VEHICLES WILL BE TOWED
AND STORED AT OWNER'S
EXPENSE. C.V.C. #22658

Miracle **FUCK**

# let's FUCK

**Come to the student forum on Monday, November 20, 8 P.M.**

**Mac 109**

*Chapel credit will be given.*
**Hosted by GCSA**

ELIZABETH GRADY

FACE FUCK

REAR of BUILDING

FUCK BRAIN

HAIRDRESSIN

ROAST MEAT FUCK RD

CREAM FUCK D

DEAD END

DOG FUCK LA

THE JAMES BOND FUCK COLLECTION

1

007

ASTON MARTIN DB5

FUCK FINGER

TECHNICAL ANAL FUCK

RESIDENTIAL & COMMERCIAL

FUCKING

(718)748-4549

$15 per man

2 hour minimum

LOCAL & LONG DISTANCE & LAST MINUTE

MOVING
$15 PER MAN per hour
PER TRUCK per hour
2 man & 2 hours minimum
SAME PRICE
7 DAYS A WEEK
718-748-4549

MOVING
$15 PER MAN per hour
PER TRUCK per hour
2 man & 2 hours minimum
SAME PRICE
7 DAYS A WEEK
718-748-4549

MOVING
$15 PER MAN per hour
PER TRUCK per hour
2 man & 2 hours minimum
SAME PRICE
7 DAYS A WEEK
718-748-4549

WE ARE INTERESTED IN YOUR COMMENTS
ABOUT HOW THIS CITY PARK IS MANAGED AND
WHAT WE CAN DO TO BETTER **FUCK** YOU
CALL US AT 646-8911

REGLAMENTO

PRIVATE
RESTRICTED PARKING AREA
BY STICKER ONLY

VIOLATORS WILL
BE **FUCK**ED AT THEIR
OWN EXPENSE
PER MANAGEMENT

minute timer

SELF **FUCK** ING OVEN

LIFT HERE FOR LOCK LEVER

THOMSONS LAKE
PRIVATE ESTATE

A place to **FUCK**

RICHARDNOBLE

Wii

FUCK

We will be

FUCKed

Jan. 1st

**FROM:** Sarah (who loves Paul), New York, NY

Enhanced for the Visually **FUCK**ed

Please Return (FUCK)ing Carts Here Thank You

REMOVAL OF SHOPPING CART FROM THESE PREMISES IS PROHIBITED BY LAW C-22435.2

Employees Must
Wash Hands
Before Returning
to **FUCK**

1. Wet   2. Soap   3. Wash for 20 sec.   4. Rinse   5. Dry   6. Turn Off Water with paper towel

AL PACINO
**FUCK** FACE

**FUCK** deep and come often. You're one of the folks.

FROM: Sarah (who loves Paul), New York, NY

95BFM PRESENTS:

# STIFF LITTLE FUCKERS

FUCK

AUCKLAND: POWERSTATION / BAR RETRO
WEDNESDAY 14TH MAY

TICKETS ON SALE NOW FROM TICKETEK & REAL GROOVY

The hottest **FUCK** ever.

Jalapeño
Cheese Dog

Cheese
Dog    Wetzel
Dog

Wetzel's
Pretzels

BE STREET WISE
AND
**FUCK** SAFELY

FUCK

BUTTS

**DANGER**

RIP
CURRENTS

危險的 退潮流
Corrientes Peligrosas
Опасные околодонные течения

PEOPLE SWIMMING
AND **FUCK**ING HAVE
DROWNED HERE
EMERGENCY: 911

NATIONAL PARK SERVICE

BĚD

& BREAKFAST

FUCK

*lessons*

*given*

SOHO
LANDLADIES ASSOC.

6pence with potluck

2pence for horse FUCK in

No more than five
to sleep in one bed

No boots to be worn in b

NEW YORK POST

CENTS

LATE CITY FINAL

NESDAY, DECEMBER 26, 2007 / Afternoon rain, 48 / Weather: Page 16 ★★

25¢

www.nypost.com

# Tiger terror

## FUCKs visitor at zoo cafe

SEE PAGE 5

This is Tatiana, the tiger that killed a young man at the San Francisco Zoo.

FROM: Sarah (who loves Paul), New York, NY

When did you last **FUCK** your dog?

STOP WORMS DEAD

# CAUTION

DO NOT FUCK ON, IN, OR AROUND THIS CONTAINER

A602

ScreenTech 1-800-829-3021

FROM: Cody

IM FIELD
CLOSED
FOR
MAINTENANCE
———————
PLEASE ~~STAY~~ FUCK OFF
THE FIELD

BILL'S
GONE FUCKING

Think you can do better?

**FUCK**thiswebsite.com

Get stickers. Send photos.